Animal Watch

Overview

Human responses to animals are largely cultural. Children from different backgrounds may see the same dog as a cute pet, a work animal, or a menace. This theme shows a variety of animals, wild and domestic, in typical settings. The first selection, *Losing Leo*, is a touching story of a lost cat. The nonfiction reading, *Animals Don't Wear Pajamas*, describes the sleeping habits of wild animals. The magazine piece presents fascinating animal facts, articles, and pictures.

Animal Watch helps children acquire competency in English while learning to appreciate diverse cultural attitudes toward animals. Key vocabulary words emphasize animal types, animal behavior, and pet care. Language structures include contractions, adverbs, and plurals. Reading strategies include contrasting textual and pictorial points of view, skimming for main ideas, and scanning for information. Practical language includes expressing feelings, giving compliments, giving, accepting, and declining invitations, and saying good night. Writing tasks for this theme include writing a news article, a slogan or advertisement, and creating a book jacket with a brief book review.

Planning Ahead: The Theme Project

Tell children they will create a Classroom Zoo where they can show what they have learned about animals. Start the project by inviting them to bring in representations of favorite animals (stuffed, those that children have made, pictures of animals cut from magazines, or other kinds of likenesses). Encourage children to share what they know about "their animal," including where it lives, what it eats, and how it sounds and moves. (Example: A student who brings in a stuffed tiger may explain that tigers are big cats that live in Asia.) Children will work on their own, with partners, and in small groups to arrange their stuffed animals and animal pictures in a "zoo." Start by encouraging children to think of zoos they are familiar with. You might bring in photos of animals in different zoo environments. Have children imagine that they are zoo animals. Ask them what would they need to make them healthy and happy.

Getting Ready to Read

Theme Presentation

What Do Children Know?

Explain to children that they will be talking, reading, and writing about animals. To discover what prior knowledge children have about pets and what they can express in English, ask questions such as these:

▶ *Act like an animal you know.* (PREPRODUCTION)

▶ *Do you like pets, or not?* (EARLY PRODUCTION)

▶ *What kind of pet would you like to have?* (SPEECH EMERGENCE)

▶ *Why do you (don't you) like pets?* (NEARLY-FLUENT)

What Do Children Want to Know?

Invite children to name animals they have seen as pets. List the animals in a chart. Discuss why those animals make good pets and add the reasons to the middle column. If students feel some animals wouldn't make good pets, have them add their reasons to the righthand column.

Animal	Reasons It Would Make a Good Pet	Reasons It Wouldn't Make a Good Pet
dog	friendly, fun to play with	bites, barks
bird	pretty	flies away
snake	exciting	bites

Display the chart and invite children to add more animals and reasons as they work.

OBJECTIVES

● **READING** To activate background knowledge
● **LISTENING/SPEAKING** To name types of pets/To describe activities with pets
● **WRITING** To describe a pet
● **CULTURAL** To appreciate diverse cultural attitudes about pets

KEY VOCABULARY

dog, puppy, cat, kitten, fish, hamster, rabbit, chicken, pony, duck, wash, brush, pet, feed, clean, veterinarian

Introduce

▶ If practical, bring an animal to class. Be prepared to deal with students' varied feelings about animals. For example, some cultures may view hamsters and gerbils as rats. Reassure students that the animal is friendly and safe. Encourage students to interact gently with the animal and to talk about it and to it, but never to tease it.

▶ Show Transparency 1 and encourage volunteers to point to the pictures and either name the pets or tell what is happening in each one. You may wish to use the following to initiate students' comments.

Point to the cat and kittens. (P)*
Are the people riding or petting the pony? (EP)*
What animals are at the pet show? (SE)*
Which animals do you know best? How do you know them? (NF)*

▶ Invite volunteers to describe in more detail what they see in each picture. Paraphrase comments in standard English if necessary, and repeat main information to help less fluent students understand.

Practice

Have less fluent students do Activity Page 1 in small groups; more fluent students can do it independently or in pairs. The writing activity at the bottom of the page extends the activity for more advanced students. You may also use Story Card 1 and its questions geared for four levels of language acquisition.

Evaluate

Confer with less fluent students about their work on Activity Page 1. They should be able to name the animals. Meet with more fluent students over the next few days to discuss what they wrote and to evaluate how much they are able to expand on the writing topic in conversation.

LITERATURE PART 1 FICTION **Getting Ready to Read**

Look at the pictures. Name some animals that make good pets. Tell what you would do to care for them.

dog	cat	rabbit	duck	pet
puppy	kitten	chicken	wash	feed
pony	fish	hamster	brush	clean

PET SHOW

VETERINARIAN

2   Animal Watch

Preview · *Losing Leo*

OBJECTIVES

- **READING** To explore the content of a story using the text and pictures/To skim for main ideas
- **LISTENING/SPEAKING** To describe pictures/To tell how a story ends/To express feelings
- **WRITING** To sequence the events of a story/ To write an ending to a story/To make a time line

KEY VOCABULARY

diary, road, gas station, worst, nowhere, lost, smart, hope, wish, find, walk, try, drown

Look at each picture and read each sentence.
Then make up an ending to the story.

Vocabulary Preview

▶ Display Transparency 2 on the overhead projector, covering the sentences. Spark a discussion about the scene by asking questions such as the following:

Where is the dog? Point to him. **(P)***
Is the dog running or walking? **(EP)***
In the last picture, where do you think the dog is trying to go? **(SE)***
Why is the dog walking down the road? **(NF)***

⊞ Have students describe the pictures and guess what is happening in the story. Then uncover the sentences at the bottom of the transparency. Have volunteers read the sentences aloud. Then invite students to match each sentence to one of the pictures, putting the text in sequence. Children may work in small groups to decide the order of the sentences. In each group, one student may serve as scribe to write the sentences in order. Then have each group work together to make up an ending for the story. Invite representatives from each group to read their story endings to the class. Encourage discussion about the different endings.

Looking Ahead

Have students open to page 4 and let them notice that each page is written in diary form. Then have them skim the first sentence on each page except the last. (Keep the ending a surprise!) Have children make predictions about the story based on their preview. Jot down their predictions on chart paper or on the board.

*Language Acquisition Levels: P = PREPRODUCTION;
EP = EARLY PRODUCTION; SE = SPEECH EMERGENCE;
NF = NEARLY-FLUENT

HOME–SCHOOL CONNECTION

Discuss with children the different ways people use animals, such as for transportation, for work, and for food. Have children take home Activity Page 2. (You may wish to have this page translated into languages not provided by the publisher.) Encourage students to talk with family members about the roles of animals in their home cultures. Invite students to talk about their work when they bring the pages back to class.

Rereading for Different Purposes

Reading the story several times will help students understand the content, vocabulary, and format. Guide students to set a different purpose for each reading.

▶ Invite students to tell how they might feel if their pet were lost. Have students find passages that show the narrator's feelings.

▶ Children can read the story to track the cat's progress home. They can make a time line from April 9 to May 6 and talk about what might have happened between May 2 and May 5.

▶ Invite children to listen to the audio tape and follow along in the book. Encourage students to read aloud with the tape, focusing on the pronunciation of new words as they read.

Reading the Literature

Losing Leo

Introduce

Explain to students that they are going to read a story about a cat that gets lost and tries to find its way home. Discuss the idea that many people write in a diary to tell their personal thoughts and feelings. The diary is often written in letter form. Explain that the entire story they are about to read is in this form. Write a brief diary entry on the board, telling about today. Read it aloud or have a volunteer do so. Then tell students to keep a diary in their journal, making one entry each day as they study *Losing Leo*.

Read

▶ Students will gradually discover that there are two levels to this story. The pictures show the cat, Leo, at large. The text shows Leo's owner's diary, a first-person narrative. The narrator does not see the events shown in the pictures, but can only wonder what is happening to Leo. To highlight this point of view, have students read the first page and ask them, *Who is speaking?*

▶ Read the story aloud to the class. Pause at the end of each page and invite volunteers to summarize what they heard. Encourage them to focus on the main idea of each page.

▶ Encourage students to guess the meanings of new words from context. To reinforce comprehension, have volunteers provide synonyms for key words.

On This Page

▶ To help students understand the colloquial expression *lickety split*, snap your fingers. Explain that something that happens *lickety split* happens as quickly as a snap of the fingers.

▶ To help set the mood for the story, ask students how the narrator seems to be feeling. *(sad)*

▶ Invite students to call for Leo, as the narrator and her family did. Encourage children to use a variety of words or sounds from English and their home languages.

▶ Have children predict what they think might happen to Leo next. Encourage children to back up their predictions with specific details from this page.

Language Focus

● *Have to* and *had to*

Point out that *have to* means "needs to" or "must." Then write the following sentences on the board:

We have to leave now.
We must leave now.
We don't have to leave now.

Ask students to tell which sentences mean the same thing. Then ask them to say the sentence that means the opposite. Explain that in *Losing Leo*, the past tense *had to* is used several times.

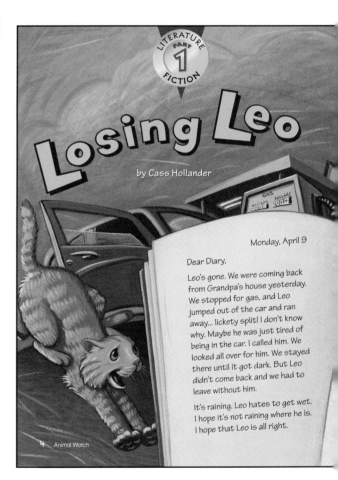

LITERATURE
PART
1
FICTION

Losing Leo

by Cass Hollander

Monday, April 9

Dear Diary,

Leo's gone. We were coming back from Grandpa's house yesterday. We stopped for gas, and Leo jumped out of the car and ran away... lickety split! I don't know why. Maybe he was just tired of being in the car. I called him. We looked all over for him. We stayed there until it got dark. But Leo didn't come back and we had to leave without him.

It's raining. Leo hates to get wet. I hope it's not raining where he is. I hope that Leo is all right.

4 Animal Watch

Meeting Individual Needs

REINFORCEMENT

▶ *Logical/mathematical* learners may better understand the narrator's feelings by calculating how many days pass from April 9, when Leo is lost, to May 6, when Leo returns home.

▶ Have children explain how they would feel if their pet were lost. Urge them to use feeling words, such as *sad, worried,* and *unhappy.* Then ask how the pet would feel if it were lost. Guide them to use additional feeling words such as *scared* and *lonely.* Write the words on the

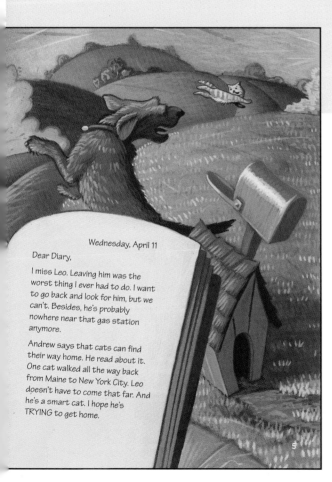

Wednesday, April 11

Dear Diary,

I miss Leo. Leaving him was the worst thing I ever had to do. I want to go back and look for him, but we can't. Besides, he's probably nowhere near that gas station anymore.

Andrew says that cats can find their way home. He read about it. One cat walked all the way back from Maine to New York City. Leo doesn't have to come that far. And he's a smart cat. I hope he's TRYING to get home.

board and have children use them to summarize what they have read thus far.

▶ To focus in on the strong bonds people often form with their pets, you may want to use the picture and questions on Story Card 2.

BUILDING SELF-ESTEEM

Ask small groups of students of mixed fluency levels to work together to answer the question *If you were lost and far from home, how would you get back?* Students may work in English and their home languages to brainstorm a list of strategies, tips, and suggestions from personal experience and imagination. Virtually all children have either been lost or have imagined being lost. ESL students are especially

On This Page

▶ Read aloud the first paragraph on page 5. Ask students how the girl seems to feel. Why? *(sad; she doesn't think she will ever see Leo again)* Then read the next paragraph. Ask if the girl seems to have more hope now that Leo will come home. Why? *(Andrew told her that cats can find their way home.)*

▶ After reading this page, have students look again at the picture. Remind them of the diary writer's point of view by asking *Who is writing the diary?*

likely to be proud of their survival skills in unfamiliar environments.

CHALLENGE

Invite more fluent students to make up the missing diary entry for April 10. Guide these children to brainstorm Leo's adventures during that day. Here are some prompts you may wish to use:

Where did Leo go when he first ran away? Where was he during the day? At night? Where did he sleep?

Children can read their diary entries to a group of classmates or record them. Invite listeners to question the storytellers about their reasons for selecting the events they chose. You may also use this activity for less fluent students by having them draw what Leo did on April 10.

Then ask *Can the narrator see what is happening to Leo?* By comparing the diary entry to the picture, they will discover the double-strand nature of the story. At times the pictures confirm the narration, as in the sentence, "I hope he's TRYING to get home." At other times, the narrator can't guess what's happening to Leo, as on page 7, when the narrator despairs of Leo's return. That's the fun of the story!

▶ Ask students why the word *trying* is written in capital letters on page 5. Invite volunteers to read the sentence aloud, stressing the word *trying* to show that it is being emphasized.

Cross-Curricular Connections

LANGUAGE ARTS/MULTICULTURAL

Invite students to tell briefly how the sounds of common animals are expressed in their home languages. In English and other languages, compare the sounds made by such animals as a cow, a sheep, a dog, a rooster, a horse, and a cat. Be sure to name the languages they represent, too. Then invite children to say the names of common pets and other animals in their home languages. Have children share these names with their classmates.

SCIENCE

Invite students to find out how animals adapt for survival in harsh weather conditions. During cold winters, animals may hibernate, grow thicker pelts, or develop white coloring as camouflage. Even pets such as cats and dogs adapt to changes in weather. Encourage students to use their knowledge of animals from their home countries and to find more information in the school library.

Mainstream Connections

Encourage children to share with mainstream peers their research about animal survival in extreme weather conditions.

Language Focus

- **Contractions and apostrophes**
- ▶ Remind students that in a contraction an apostrophe takes the place of a letter or letters that are left out. Then create a chart like the one below to show some common contractions.

Contraction	Spelled-Out Words	Letter Left Out
couldn't	could not	o
Leo's	Leo is	i
doesn't	does not	o

- ▶ Ask students to find other contractions in the story. (*don't, it's, didn't, he's*)

Story Card 1

On These Pages

- ▶ Children may be unfamiliar with the word *cupboard*. Point to a cupboard in your classroom, if possible, and explain that it is a *closet with shelves*.
- ▶ In the sentence "It's been too long," be sure students understand that *long* refers to time, not distance.

Saturday, April 15

Dear Diary,

I watched a movie last night about two dogs and a cat who found their way home. They had to go over the mountains. It seemed to take them forever. The cat almost drowned. One of the dogs fell into a big hole and couldn't get out. But they made it. It was such a great movie. But it made me miss Leo even more.

I hope Leo's trying to get home. I hope he doesn't fall in any big holes. I miss him so much.

Theme Project Update

As students come to the end of *Losing Leo*, help them consider how they could use the information from the story in planning their classroom zoo. To spark ideas, present students with these possibilities:

- Have children brainstorm a list of animals to include in their zoo. Have them decide if they want to have animals from all over the world or animals from just a certain part of the world.
- Children can design homes for each of the animals that keep them not only safe, but also healthy and happy. Instead of cages and bars, children might want to use natural boundaries, such as mountains, walls, and lakes. Encourage students to read in English or their first language about the animals that interest them and to find out the natural habitats of the animals.
- Have students make a poster advertising their new zoo. The poster should include the name of the zoo, the animals that live there, where the zoo is located, and when the zoo opens.
- Suggest that children make a map so that visitors can find their way around the zoo. Less fluent children can use their visual map-making skills and also label the map.

Everyday Talk

● **Expressing feelings**

The narrator of *Losing Leo* expresses powerful feelings about a missing cat. Tell students that we all have feelings and sometimes we need to tell about them—to express them. Ask, *What are some ways that you feel? When do you feel them?* After the first couple of answers (perhaps *happy* and *sad*) ask, *What other feelings do you know?* (*worried, excited, lonely,* etc.) *What do you say to express feelings? What do you say to ask about someone's feelings?* As it emerges in discussion, write this question-and-answer pattern on the board: *How are you? How are you feeling? I'm feeling_____.* Model an exchange based on that pattern with a nearly-fluent student. Have students form pairs to practice the exchange. More fluent students can add the question *Why?* and practice giving explanations.

Monday, May 1

Dear Diary,

I put Leo's cat dish away in the cupboard. I don't think he's coming home. It's been too long. If he were coming home, he would be here by now.

I hope Leo has a place to live. Maybe he found nice people to take care of him. He was such a good cat, and I loved him so much. I wish I knew what happened to him.

Direct children to the chart they began before they read this story. Invite volunteers to read the original listings and any words they added as they read *Losing Leo.* Review all the words. Ask students to tell what they learned about pets and their owners in this story. Discuss how people feel about their pets. Students may want to add more animals, and the reasons they make good pets, to the chart.

WRITER'S JOURNAL

- Have students write how they think Leo feels about being home again.
- Have students write at least one more sentence for the narrator's diary of May 6.
- Suggest that students write about an experience they have had with a pet or other animal. They may describe their feelings toward the animal or how they resolved a problem. Less proficient writers may use drawings to help tell their story.

After You Read

Post-Reading Activities

Vocabulary Check

▶ Have students review the pictures of children and their pets on page 2 and Transparency 1. Invite less fluent students to name all the animals they can, and encourage them to describe the scenes in brief phrases. Guide more fluent students to describe the scenes in imaginative detail, using questions such as *Why do you think the puppy needs to go to the doctor?* and *What do you think is going to happen to those kittens?*

▶ Reinforce animal names by having children play Animal Charades. Model the game for students by soundlessly pretending to be an animal and having students guess its identity. Then have a series of volunteers act out animals of their choice. Encourage discussion and debate among the guessers. If students have trouble guessing, allow the players to make animal sounds while pantomiming.

Comprehension Check

▶ Have children do the After You Read activity in pairs or individually. Point out that their calendars help complete the story by showing the experiences Leo was having that the narrator did not know about. Have students summarize the story, including details from both the narrator's diary and their own calendars.

▶ For further practice, you can use the transparencies and story cards from the Set I theme booklet *Animals, Animals*. These include farm animals and a pet shop.

Practice

Now that students have read *Losing Leo*, their new vocabulary and understanding of the narrative should permit them to make up more extensive, original endings for the story of Paco the dog on page 3. Show Transparency 2 again and invite them to stretch their imaginations to make up exciting, funny, unpredictable, or silly endings.

Looking Back at the Story

▶ You may wish to conduct a round-robin retelling of the story. Arrange students in a circle and have each child provide one sentence of the summary, picking up where the previous speaker left off.

▶ Invite children to become reporters and investigate Leo's disappearance. Tell them that reporters have a special way of remembering the questions they need answered—they use the "5W's and H." Write each initial and the corresponding word on the board.

Who?	What?
When	Where?
Why?	How?

▶ As a class, use a 5W's-and-H chart to gather story details about Leo's disappearance.

Saturday, May 6

Dear Diary,
LEO'S BACK! He made it!

Evaluate

Have students refer back to the story of Paco the dog on page 3. Now that students have read about both Paco and Leo, ask, *How is Paco different from Leo?* Less fluent students, using phrases or single words, should be able to point out rudimentary similarities and differences. Examples: *Both were lost and later found. Paco is a dog and Leo is a cat.* More fluent students should be able to compare and contrast details from the two stories. You may wish to rate students' answers relative to their language acquisition level by using a simple rubric, such as +, ✓, −.

After You Read

Here is a calendar that shows April 9 through May 6, the time that Leo was missing.

APRIL

Sunday	Monday	Tuesday	Wednesday	Thursday	Friday	Saturday
		1	2	3	4	5
6	7	8	9	10	11	12
13	14	15	16	17	18	19
20	21	22	23	24	25	26
27	28	29	30			

MAY

Sunday	Monday	Tuesday	Wednesday	Thursday	Friday	Saturday
				1	2	3
4	5	6	7	8	9	10
11	12	13	14	15	16	17

On a separate sheet of paper, write what you think Leo did each day he was gone. Look back at the story to help you. Remember: Leo must reach home on May 6.

9

WRITER'S CORNER

Beginning

- **To dictate a story or a letter**
- **To copy written material**

PRE-WRITE: Remind children that Grandpa doesn't know that Leo ran away. Tell them that together they will write a letter to Grandpa about it. WRITE: At the upper lefthand corner of the board, write *Dear Grandpa.* Then invite students to suggest sentences that they would like to write Grandpa about Leo's disappearance. Put all the suggestions into the letter on the board, paraphrasing into standard English when necessary. REVISE, EDIT: Edit at the board, with students making changes as a group. Have them reread the letter silently. Then ask them if its meaning is clear and how to change the words where the meaning isn't clear. Ask if the sentence order is good. As a last step, invite students to check spelling and mechanics. Then have them each recopy the letter on paper and let a partner check it for errors. PUBLISH: Invite beginning writers to read their letters to one or more classmates.

Intermediate

- **To make a word bank**
- **To write a diary entry**

PRE-WRITE: Invite children to create a brief diary entry about a real or imagined pet and its care. Students should start by making a word bank consisting of the types of animals and the words describing their care, such as *brushing* and *feeding.* WRITE:

Have students write their entries in diary form. Remind children to include a date and the "Dear Diary" heading. REVISE, EDIT: Have students trade with partners to read each other's diaries and make constructive suggestions. PUBLISH: Children can add an illustration and post their finished entries on the bulletin board.

Advanced

- **To use a 5*W*'s-and-*H* chart to pre-write**
- **To write a news article**

PRE-WRITE: Ask students to write a news article about the events in *Losing Leo.* The article might ask readers to be on the lookout for the lost cat, or it might describe the cat's return. Have them review the charts they filled out for Looking Back at the Story as well as the narrator's diary entries. Invite them to ask themselves, *What's the most important fact in my article?* WRITE: Have students begin their articles with the most important fact and include as many 5*W*'s-and-*H* facts as possible in their stories. Also have them include a headline and a byline. REVISE, EDIT: Have partners serve as news editors to read their reporters' copy, pencil in comments, and request revisions. PUBLISH: Have students lay out mock news articles on a computer or by hand, and post them on the bulletin board or distribute them to classmates.

For coordinating activities, see the CD-ROM disk that corresponds with this theme.

Getting Ready to Read

What Do Children Know?

Tell children that some animals are happier in nature than they are indoors. Explain that students will read about wild animals that live in the woods, on the plains, and in the oceans. Initially you may want to allow students to use their first languages to tell you what they know about some wild animals. Say:

▶ *Show me an elephant.* **(P)***

▶ *Which is bigger, a lion or a cat?* **(EP)***

▶ *What is the difference between a lion and a cat?* **(SE)***

▶ *If you could be a wild animal, what would you be? Why?* **(NF)***

What Do Children Want to Know?

Begin a chart by eliciting from children the names of wild animals they know. If some children can tell about wild animals only in their first languages, ask others for the English equivalent and add it to the chart. Brainstorm facts that students already know about the animals and questions that they are curious about for a chart like this one:

Animal	We know...	We want to know...
elephant	very big has trunk	How much does an elephant eat?
bear	very strong	Are all bears mean?
wolf	like a dog	Where do wolves live?

Invite students to add animal names and information to the chart as they read.

Theme Presentation

OBJECTIVES

● **READING** To activate background knowledge/To generate vocabulary in context

● **LISTENING/SPEAKING** To tell about experiences/To respond to questions

KEY VOCABULARY

wild animal, habitat, plain, elephant, lion, zebra, hyena, crocodile, bear, mountain goat, sea otter, beaver

Introduce

▶ Display Transparency 3 or page 10, which shows some wild animals, their habitats, and daytime activities. Start by asking children to name the animals as you or they point to them.

▶ Explain that the place in which an animal usually lives is its *habitat.* Have volunteers name some habitats. *(mountains, hills, plains, rivers, oceans)* Build on the discussion by inviting children to answer the following:

Where's the mountain? Where's a goat? **(PREPRODUCTION)**
Does the bear live in the mountains or on the plains? **(EARLY PRODUCTION)**
Which animals live on the plains? Where could those plains be? **(SPEECH EMERGENCE)**
Why do you think so many animals live on the plains of Africa? **(NEARLY-FLUENT)**

▶ Point out that in real life all these animals do not live on the same continent. The plains could be in Africa, and the mountains could be in North America.

▶ Encourage students to describe the activities that animals do during the day. List the action words on the board under

Daytime Activities. (hunt, play, eat, care for young)

Practice

Have students do Activity Page 3 independently. Then join partners to compare their efforts and to offer help to each other.

Evaluate

Use the activity page to evaluate informally less fluent students' ability to use new vocabulary in familiar contexts. Ask questions such as, *What animal is this? Where do you see the word* bear? The activity can be used with more fluent students to compare speaking versus writing competency in English. You may wish to keep notes for future reference.

Getting Ready to Read

Animals by Day and Night

wild animal	elephant	hyena	beaver
habitat	lion	crocodile	mountain goat
plain	zebra	bear	sea otter

10   Animal Watch

Preview • *Animals Don't Wear Pajamas*

wolf	giraffe	sleep	hunt	lie down
pup	gorilla	float	care for	stand up
cub	den	fly	curl up	wake up

11

Vocabulary Preview

▶ Display Transparency 4 and elicit that it shows what different animals do at night. Tell children that animals, like people, have different bedtimes and different ways of sleeping. Have children study the transparency. Try to lead them to make observations about the sleep habits of different animals by asking questions such as: *Do all animals sleep at night? Where do animals sleep? (in dens, trees) How do they sleep? (lying down, standing, floating)* Adapt the questions to reflect your students' ability to provide answers.

▶ Point to one of the habitat "zones" and ask students to look at particular animals, such as the family of wolves sleeping in a hollow log or the bear in its den. Encourage students to describe what they see and to use visual clues to draw conclusions about the animal. For example, bears live in dens and sleep for long periods each winter. Repeat the process for other animals.

Looking Ahead

Have students preview the text and illustrations. Then ask them the following questions: *Do you see any animals that you know? Which ones? Do you see any animals that you don't know?* Invite students to compare the pictures and the selection title. Ask students why they think the author chose to use the title *Animals Don't Wear Pajamas.* Chart students' comments to use after the reading.

> * Language Acquisition Levels: P = PREPRODUCTION;
> EP = EARLY PRODUCTION; SE = SPEECH EMERGENCE;
> NF = NEARLY-FLUENT

Reading the Literature

Animals Don't Wear Pajamas

Introduce

▶ Point to the classroom clock and ask how it helps us know when to go to sleep and when to wake up.

▶ Inform students that people and animals have inner clocks, or biological clocks, that tell them when to sleep and when to awaken. Most often, a "clock" of this kind runs in cycles of approximately twenty-four hours. Some animals sleep at night and are awake during the daytime, and some do the opposite. Invite students to mention the times they prefer to go to bed and to wake up.

Read

▶ Begin by asking children to scan the first sentence of each page or paragraph to find out which animal is being discussed.

▶ After they have identified each animal discussed on a page, children should skim the rest of the page to find one or two important facts that are presented in the section.

▶ Read aloud the complete story for students' enjoyment without interrupting the reading to ask them questions. Students may not understand every word, but they should listen to grasp as much as possible.

▶ Since this reading has words that students may not understand from context, the selection can be used to help students develop dictionary skills. For those who may be unfamiliar with the use of an English dictionary, point out the importance of first determining the base word (*bulge*, not *bulging*), using the guide words at the tops of pages to locate the word, and finding the appropriate meaning if there is more than one given.

On This Page

After the initial reading, have students reread for details and to develop a deeper comprehension. Notice which words on this page gave them trouble. Explain that when they don't know the meaning of a word, they should follow the strategy of using the illustrations and the rest of the sentence or the paragraph to help them figure out the meaning. Ask how reading the first sentence would help them figure out what pajamas are. Use a similar procedure for words in the paragraph about hummingbirds.

Language Focus

● **Plural nouns**

Explain that words that name more than one person, place, or thing are called *plural nouns*. Tell children that most plural nouns end in *s* or *es*. Then have students point out the plural nouns on this page. (*animals, clocks, pajamas, hummingbirds, lots, birds, wings*) Remind them that not every word ending in *s* is a noun or a plural noun. (Examples: *its, falls, backwards, sideways*)

Animals don't wear pajamas, and they don't have ticking clocks to tell them when it's time to go to sleep. But animals do know when it's time to rest.

When darkness falls, it's time for hummingbirds to sleep. They need lots of rest after a full day of darting forwards, backwards, and sideways. During the day these tiny birds flap their wings so fast that the wings seem to disappear. All night long they sit perfectly still in a deep sleep. They won't move again until sunrise.

12 Animal Watch

Meeting Individual Needs

REINFORCEMENT

Kinesthetic learners will enjoy doing a series of creative movement studies of the animal kingdom. Have them decide what animals to be and enact how their animals live, act, hunt, care for their young, and then fall asleep. Encourage children to reread each page, then review the class chart to find words that describe each animal's habits. The hummingbird's daytime wing movements and darting around might be contrasted to its sitting still while sleeping.

BUILDING SELF-ESTEEM

Have children present the songs, stories, and other materials that they researched for the Home-School Connection on Teacher's Edition page 11. You may want to adapt the presentations in the following ways: children who bring in songs might sing them "live" or play audio tapes of others singing them; children who bring in stories might use drawings to tell the stories or they might act them out. Encourage students to talk about the materials they found and where they found them. Consider taping their performances and displaying their stories and artwork on the bulletin board.

CHALLENGE

Have interested students create a Sleep Studies Center where they can exhibit information, photographs, and drawings about the sleep habits of animals found in their native countries and in other parts of the world. Launch the center by bringing in books on the subject from the school library. The full-length version of *Animals Don't Wear Pajamas* is a place to start. Other good sources are *Do Not Disturb* by Margery Facklam, Sierra Club Books/Little, Brown, 1989, and *Elephants Can't Jump* by Barbara Seuling, Dutton, 1985. An encyclopedia is another valuable source.

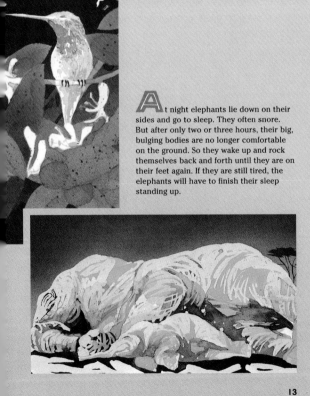

At night elephants lie down on their sides and go to sleep. They often snore. But after only two or three hours, their big, bulging bodies are no longer comfortable on the ground. So they wake up and rock themselves back and forth until they are on their feet again. If they are still tired, the elephants will have to finish their sleep standing up.

13

On This Page

- ▶ Explain that some animals and people make a noise called *snoring* when they sleep. Have volunteers demonstrate.
- ▶ Help children deal with the word *bulging*. If less fluent children understand that elephants don't sleep well because they are so big, point out that they do not need to know the exact meaning of *bulging*. Encourage others to guess at a meaning; they may say *baggy* or *lumpy*. Nearly-fluent readers who are trying to build vocabulary may want to keep a word list and consult a dictionary.
- ▶ Ask a volunteer to demonstrate rocking back and forth. If no student can, demonstrate the action for the class.

Story Card 3

Cross-Curricular Connections

SOCIAL STUDIES/ART

Explain to children that the elephant and the sea otter are endangered animals—animals that are in danger of dying out. Have children choose one of the animals and then work together in small groups to create a poster that appeals to people to help save their animal. Encourage children to include both words and pictures in their posters. Display the posters in the classroom or around the school. Endangered animals are also shown in story cards, transparencies, and the theme poster for Part 2 of *Taking Care of the Earth* in Set III of this series.

HEALTH

How important is sleep to a person's health? To raise children's awareness of the importance of getting sufficient sleep, discuss the issue. You may want to start by asking questions such as the following: *What time do you go to bed? Do you go to bed every night at the same time? How do you feel when you don't get enough sleep? Why is it important to get enough sleep every night?*

MATH

Talk with children about the different amounts of sleep needed by each animal discussed in this book. Male lions, for example, may sleep as much as

twenty-two hours a day! What about individual children—how much sleep do *they* need? Invite everyone to keep a record for one week of how long they sleep each night. They should note the time they went to sleep at night and the time they awakened in the morning. At the end of the week, create a class chart showing how much sleep children in the class got every night. Have volunteers point out the least amount and the most amount of sleep a child got, and then calculate the average number of hours each child slept during the week.

MUSIC/MULTICULTURAL

Parents around the world sing to their children to induce sleep. Invite volunteers to share lullabies from their home countries. You may want to tape-record the songs and place them in the class library.

Mainstream Connections

Suggest that students share their animal posters with friends in their mainstream classes and discuss with them why it is important to help save the sea otter and the elephant. Ask permission from their classroom teachers to exhibit the posters.

On This Page

Ask students to provide a synonym for the word *cubs*. Then ask them to find the word for baby wolves (*pups*, page 16).

You might also present the names given to the young of other animals, such as *kitten* (cat), *puppy* (dog), *kid* (goat), *calf* (cow), *colt* (horse).

Language Focus

● **Adverbs**

Write these questions on chart paper: *Where? When? How? How much?* An *adverb* answers one of the four questions. Tell the class that many adverbs, like *usually*, end in *-ly*. Other adverbs, for example *alone*, have different endings. Point out that *alone* tells us how the male lion sleeps and *usually* tells us when he sleeps alone. Suggest that more fluent students find more adverbs and make up questions to be answered by the rest of the class. (Example: *How do hummingbirds flap their wings?*)

L ions sleep both day and night. Male lions usually sleep alone, and they may sleep as much as twenty-two out of twenty-four hours! Female lions spend most of their time with cubs and other females. They sleep less because it is their responsibility to hunt for food and care for the cubs.

14   Animal Watch

Theme Project Update

When students have completed their reading, encourage them to consider how they can integrate what they learned in *Animals Don't Wear Pajamas* with their theme project plans. Here are some suggestions for children to consider.

▶ Design each animal's habitat to support its natural sleeping patterns. Lions, for example, should have some trees in which to sleep; sea otters need seaweed to make them comfortable at night. Encourage children to look at the pages in *Animals Don't Wear Pajamas* as they design each animal's living space and to read about other animals' living spaces in library books such as *Animal Homes* by Brian Wildsmith, Oxford University Press, 1980.

▶ Children can make a sign for each animal's habitat that explains its sleeping habits. For example, a sign by the lion enclosure might say "Do not disturb. We are male lions and we need a lot of sleep—as much as twenty-two hours a day."

Everyday Talk

● **Saying good night**

▶ Ask children to imagine that they got sleepy and decided to go to bed. Elicit the home-language expressions they would use to say good night. Then ask volunteers what people say in English. Write answers, such as *good night,* on the board.

▶ Ask how people let others know they are ready to go to bed. Start by writing *I'm sleepy* on the board. Help students add other expressions they might hear such as *I'm tired and I'm going to bed.*

▶ Discuss responses to saying good night, such as *Sleep well. Sleep tight. See you tomorrow.* With a volunteer, model the following exchange:

Person 1: *I'm tired.*
Person 2: *Why don't you go to bed?*
Person 1: *I think I will. Good night.*
Person 2: *Good night. Sleep tight.*

Practice the role-play with several pairs. Then have students continue on their own.

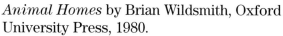
On This Page

You may want to explain that the *sway* of the sea is the natural movement of the waves and tides. Model the action of swaying back and forth.

ea otters sleep floating in the water after wrapping themselves in strands of seaweed. These seaweed ties keep the otters from drifting away with the sway of the sea.

15

What Did Children Learn?

Have children look back at the chart they started earlier in the theme. Invite volunteers to read the entries on the chart and then work as a class to complete the chart, using what they learned. Use questions such as these:

▶ *Show us what a gray wolf looks like when it sleeps.* (P)*

▶ *Do hummingbirds move or stay still when they sleep?* (EP)*

▶ *Why do sea otters wrap themselves in seaweed as they sleep?* (SE)*

▶ *Why don't female lions sleep as much as male lions?* (NF)*

WRITER'S JOURNAL

▶ Encourage students to write how they feel about the book *Animals Don't Wear Pajamas.* **Ask:** *What did you learn that you didn't know before? What was the most surprising thing you learned? What questions would you still like to find out about?*

▶ Invite students to write about their own sleeping habits or those of a pet.

HOME–SCHOOL CONNECTION

Encourage students to select one of the animals described in the book and read that section to their family. Nearly-fluent students may wish to contrast two animals.

After You Read

Post-Reading Activities

Vocabulary Check

▶ Return to Transparencies 3 and 4 and encourage students to show how much they have learned. Invite them to take turns picking an animal, describing its habitat, and talking about its day- and nighttime habits.

▶ Use Story Card 3 to check students' vocabulary acquisition. The card reinforces the theme and will allow children to recycle familiar vocabulary in contexts that are different from the context of the story. The questions on the back are appropriate to the four levels of language development.

Comprehension Check

▶ Invite children to read the riddles on page 17 and to use what they learned in *Animals Don't Wear Pajamas* to answer them. Let more fluent students work on their own. Then pair or group them with less fluent students to help the latter do the activity. Encourage more fluent students to make up new riddles about other animals shown on pages 10–11. Examples: I always wear striped pajamas (*zebra*). My neck is as tall as a tree (*giraffe*).

▶ Invite students to talk about wild animals they have seen in nature, at zoos, or on movie or television screens. Encourage less fluent students to name the animals and where they saw them;

challenge more fluent students to describe details of their experiences. Paraphrase or summarize responses to reinforce the vocabulary and increase the comprehension of all learners.

Looking Back at the Story

▶ Invite pairs to quiz each other. One child should give the name of an animal in the selection, and the other should tell the sleeping habits of that animal. (You might make this an open-book test.) Allow partners to give each other scores for the test if they wish. Suggest that they give each other extra credit for providing other information about animals' living habits.

▶ Discuss how an animal's life might be different in the wild from what it would be in a zoo and the good and bad things about those two habitats. For instance, in the wild a lion would be free and get a lot of exercise, but it would be in danger of getting shot, whereas in a zoo it would be bored but safe and well-fed.

▶ Recall with students their comments about why the author chose the story title. Ask students if their original comments still hold true or if they wish to change them.

On This Page

Ask children to show their understanding of *den* by pointing to the illustration. Children may be interested to learn other names of animal homes. (Examples: *warren, nest, lair, burrow*)

Language Focus
● **Compound words**

Review with children the concept of compound words, and explain that sometimes two or more words are used to form one word, such as *hummingbird* and *sideways*. Invite children to work in pairs to look for other compound words in the reading selection. (Examples: *newborn, sunrise, seaweed, outside, inside*)

When a gray wolf is a new father, he will curl up to sleep outside his family's den. He guards his newborn pups and their mother who sleep inside.

Animals don't wear pajamas. But animals, just like people, do have their own special ways to sleep.

16 Animal Watch

Evaluate

Invite groups of students to join you for "Book Talk" discussions in the round. Form circles based on fluency levels so that less fluent students are not overwhelmed. Initiate a discussion by asking questions such as, *What did you like about the story? What didn't you like about it?* If students wrote journal entries (see Teacher's Edition page 15), they might read them aloud.

Encourage less fluent students to reply with phrases as well as single words. For more fluent students, take the discussion into the realm of literary criticism by asking questions such as, *What would you tell the author if you met her?* You may wish to take notes to discuss students' progress with them, their parents, and other teachers.

Everyday Talk

- Giving a compliment
- Receiving a compliment

▶ Discuss the cartoon with children. Point out that when someone has given you a compliment, it is polite to say "Thank you." Have pairs of children alternate giving compliments and accepting them with thanks. Offer these sentence starters: *I like your _____./ What great_____!/ That's a nice_____.*

▶ Invite volunteers to show how compliments and acknowledgments are offered in their home cultures. Point out body language, such as eye contact and gestures.

WRITER'S CORNER

Beginning

- **To brainstorm ideas**
- **To write a slogan**

PRE-WRITE: Invite children to make bookmarks about wild animals. After showing them one or more bookmarks, brainstorm ideas for bookmark designs based on animals depicted on pages 10–11. WRITE: Invite children to design, cut out, and draw their bookmarks, leaving room for a brief text or slogan. The text might be a phrase describing an animal, an animal fact, an invitation to read about the animal, or even the name of the animal alone. Have pairs of students draft their texts on separate pieces of paper. REVISE, EDIT: Help children check each other's work. Children can then write their texts on the bookmarks. PUBLISH: Encourage children to use the bookmarks. (Some may wish to trade with others.)

Intermediate

- **To combine text and picture**
- **To write an advertisement**

PRE-WRITE: Invite children to become advertising copywriters and artists creating products, such as pajamas, breakfast cereals, vitamin tablets, sports equipment, and outerwear, that use animal motifs. Help students form groups based on their interest in specific products. WRITE: Have each team create a print ad for their product. The art and the text should feature animals. REVISE, EDIT: Have children edit one another's work. PUBLISH: Invite volunteers to read their ads to the class and give sales pitches for their products. Display all ads.

Advanced

- **To write a brief book review**
- **To create a book jacket**

PRE-WRITE: Invite partners to create a book jacket for *Animals Don't Wear Pajamas*. Explain that most book jackets include art, a brief review of the book, and information about the author. Provide book jackets to spark ideas. WRITE: Have partners write favorable opinions of the book. REVISE, EDIT: Partners can exchange papers with other pairs to make sure that the book jackets are attractive and accurate. PUBLISH: Display the book jackets.

After You Read

Who Am I?

Match each riddle to an animal picture.

I go to sleep lying down. After a few hours, I get uncomfortable, so I sleep standing up. Who am I?

I wrap myself in seaweed so I can float when I sleep. Who am I?

I sleep in a den with my pups. Who am I?

I sleep up to twenty-two hours a day. Who am I?

I stay perfectly still when I sleep. Who am I?

I wear pajamas and sleep in a bed. Who am I?

17

EVERYDAY TALK
- **Giving a compliment**
- **Receiving a compliment**

WHAT GREAT PAJAMAS YOU HAVE!

THANK YOU VERY MUCH!

Real-Life Reading

Animal News Bits

Invite students to look at pages 18 and 19. Ask them what they would like to read first. Take a poll, announce the results, and ask students to explain their choices. Discuss that when people read magazines, they scan, or quickly look through the material, pick what interests them most, then read for short periods before they begin the process all over again. Begin with the section that got the most votes.

Python Visits Shore Family

Pre-Reading Draw a snake about eight feet long, across the chalkboard. Invite children to share what they know about snakes. Ask questions such as: *Do you like or dislike snakes? Are all snakes poisonous? What would you do if you found a snake this big in your yard?*

Reading Read the article aloud and then ask volunteers to read one sentence each. Discuss the story using the 5*W*'s and *H* of journalism—*Who, What, When, Where, Why, How?* Write those words on the board and list story facts as they are volunteered. Ask volunteers to read aloud a second time. Invite each one to read a paragraph. Encourage them to express the tones of the Ortiz family and the reporter.

Post-Reading Ask the following question: *If you were the reporter, who would you interview and what would you ask?* Have pairs write lists of questions.
▶ Have groups enact the encounter between the Ortiz family, the snake, and the snake remover. Videotape the performances if possible.

Pet Classified Ads

Pre-Reading Explain that classified ads are small ads that people place in newspapers or magazines to sell things (like cars or houses) or to make announcements. Have students scan the ads here and say what they announce. *(lost and found pets)*

Reading Have a different volunteer read each ad aloud. After each ad has been read, pause so that students can respond to the ad, summarize the information, and speculate about how the pet might have been lost and what might happen to it.

Post-Reading Have small groups write lost-and-found ads for other kinds of animals they have learned about. These may be serious or quite humorous. Model each type for students.

Animal News Bits

Python Visits Shore Family

Juan and Rita Ortiz had an unexpected visitor to their shore home this weekend—an 8-foot Southern Asian python! The family's 6-month-old dog, Cuco, discovered the snake under the front porch and would not stop barking until Juan came to check on it. Rita Ortiz grabbed a flashlight and ran to help her husband when she heard him yelling, "Rita, there's a really big snake under here!"

"I don't really mind snakes, so I thought this wouldn't be any big deal," said Rita Ortiz. "Boy, was I wrong!"

The snake was taken to the animal shelter by Wildlife Removers of Deal, New Jersey. Anyone who is missing a pet python should call 555-2211 for information.

LOST CAT
Black w/one white paw and bright gray eyes. Sad child waiting for your call. REWARD! 555-1626

FOUND
West Side, Parakeet, green and yellow. Sings "Happy Birthday." Please call 555-1816 soon or my kids will keep it!

Pet Classified Ads
Read the ads. How could you help find these lost pets?

LOST SHEEPDOG
Female. Long, gray hair, blue collar, answers to "Snickers." Last seen near Riverview Shopping Mall. Call Tom at 555-4780.

LOST DOG
8-year-old Collie, tan w/red collar. Answers to Muffy. Freeport area, 555-2759

Bats Use Radar!

Pre-Reading Bring in a photo of a bat or a plastic novelty bat. Encourage students to tell what they know about bats as you chart or web the information. Explain that bats live in most parts of the world except icy polar regions and high mountains. There are hundreds of types of bats, from the bumblebee bat (about 1 inch long with a wingspan of 6 inches) to the flying fox (16 inches long with a wingspan of 6 feet).

Reading Have students look at the diagram of echolocation on page 19. Ask questions such as the following: *What does this picture show? What is the bat doing? What are the lines that go out from the bat?* Invite students to read the article to find the answers. Because the article is rich in content, students may need to reread it several times. Stop the reading to answer questions and to have volunteers paraphrase key facts.

Post-Reading Invite students to brainstorm a list of English words that rhyme with *bat,* such as *rat, cat, fat, hat, sat.*

▶ Encourage students to go to the library and bring in more bat facts and pictures. Interested groups of students may enjoy making their own book of bat facts.

Cat and Dog Riddles

Pre-Reading Talk about riddles—what makes a riddle funny? Ask whether students can sometimes, usually, or never understand riddles in English. Invite them to try these cat and dog riddles for practice.

Reading/Post-Reading Encourage partners to take turns reading the riddles to each other and guessing the answers.

▶ Children may enjoy making up their own animal riddles. If they know animal riddles in their home languages, encourage them to tell the riddles and to try to translate them.

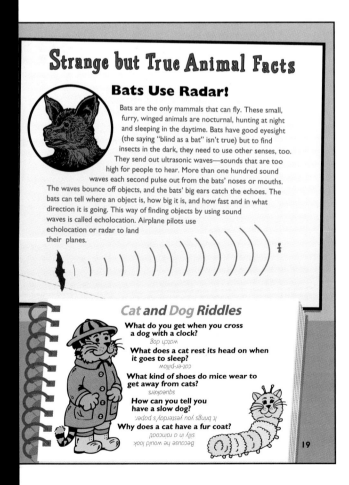

Story Card 2

Everyday Talk

- Inviting someone to do something
- Accepting or turning down an invitation

▶ Have volunteers take parts and practice the exchanges on page 20. Then talk about some situations in which we invite someone to go someplace, such as to a party, a movie, or a barbecue.

▶ Reread aloud the questions on page 20. Then have students brainstorm other ways to ask someone to go somewhere. List their suggestions on the board.

▶ Reread aloud the acceptances. Then read the rejections. Create a two-column list on the board, and write students' suggestions for other phrases they might use when saying yes or no to an invitation.

▶ Point out that when turning down an invitation it is important to be polite and considerate of the other person's feelings. Tell students that thanking the person and suggesting that they may be able to accept at another time are ways to avoid hurting feelings.

▶ With a volunteer, role-play inviting and accepting and then inviting and declining. Have other pairs role-play both circumstances for the class.

▶ Have pairs, at their seats, role-play inviting, accepting, and turning down invitations. Encourage them to use the specific situations you talked about earlier. Less fluent students might work with you or with more fluent partners. Have pairs practice until they feel confident that they can handle similar situations.

Extension Activity

On slips of paper, write sentence starters that students might say to each other to extend an invitation and to accept or reject an invitation. Put the invitations into a paper bag and the other phrases into another paper bag. Then have partners draw slips of paper, each from a different bag, and have a conversation in which one extends an invitation and the other accepts or rejects it.

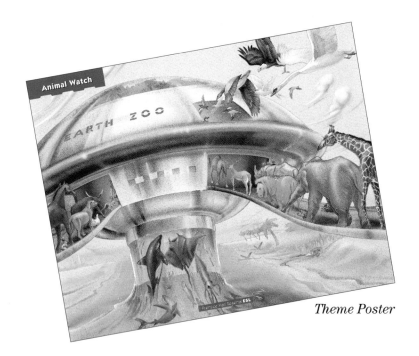

Theme Poster

Here and There

Animal Helpers

▶ Invite students to look at the illustrations on page 21 and to read the captions. Ask volunteers to describe how each animal is helping the person or people in the pictures. Encourage children to comment on the details in each illustration.

▶ On large paper, begin a chart with the following headings: Food, Work, Transportation, Friendship. Have volunteers read the headings aloud. Then discuss that these are some of the ways that animals help people. Next, under each category, have children record examples of animals that help people. Examples include the following:

Water buffaloes pull plows.
Llamas give wool.
Camels provide transportation, milk, and fibers for cloth.
Inuit dogs pull sleds.
Monkeys help disabled people by holding and bringing things.
Pet dogs, cats, and birds keep people company.

▶ Tell students about any other human-animal interactions you know about. For example, you might mention that the Aztec used Chihuahuas—small hairless dogs—to warm their feet in cold weather.

Extension Activities

▶ Have students brainstorm to come up with theories of when and how people first tamed animals. Tell them that according to one theory, prehistoric hunters brought home and raised the young of adult animals that they killed. Also, ask about differences between a wild species and its domesticated descendant: between the mountain goat and the farmyard goat, the wild boar and the hog. Ask students how they would go about trying to find the answers.

▶ No animal is more closely associated with humans than the dog. Invite students to create a photo-text display of the many breeds of dogs that have been used for work (including hunting). The list would include all the varieties of shepherds, wolfhounds, terriers, spaniels, and collies and even the poodle, which was the hunting dog of old France.

HERE AND THERE

All over the world, there are animals that live and work with people. Some are used for transportation, carrying people and goods. Other animals help people hunt or work. Some animals give milk that people drink. And some animals are sacred to the people they live among.

Desert camel caravan

Woman with guide dog

Coal miner with canary

Police with bloodhound

Do you know other ways that animals help people? Tell about them.

Horses on cattle ranches

21

Theme Project

✎ Direct children to look at the photo and illustrations on page 22. Then ask them to read aloud the directions and questions.

► Arrange children in their theme project groups, and guide them to use the questions on this page to assess their progress.

► As children work, circulate around the room to observe their progress. See whether they need any additional materials or time to complete their work.

► When everyone has finished working, have the class design an invitation. Remind children what they learned about extending an invitation in the Everyday Talk section of the text. Have students work in pairs or small groups to write the invitations and hand them out to mainstream classmates and school personnel.

Extension Activities

Invite children to make some souvenirs for visitors to their zoo. Possibilities include pennants and booklets. To make the pennants, children should glue a large paper triangle on a thin dowel. Guide them to decorate the pennant with words and pictures. The booklet might have "snapshots," maps, and other zoo memorabilia.

What You Might See
(See Theme Project Update, page 7.)

Theme Wrap-Up

Theme Game

- Guide teams in playing "Animal Wheel." Each student takes a turn, choosing to roll one die or two, three, or four dice. The student finds the place on the board that matches the number rolled and tries to name the animal shown in the place. For each correct answer the student gets one point.
- When only a few places or sections are left, deciding how many dice to roll becomes tactically important.
- Mixing proficiency levels on a team exposes less fluent students to good input from teammates. If students of the same proficiency level play together, each level would be made tougher.
- When the game is over, remind students of the many animals they studied in this theme. Remind them of the theme title, *Animal Watch.* Ask how it applies to *Losing Leo*, to *Animals Don't Wear Pajamas*, and to the magazine pages in Part 3.

Oral Review

- Use Story Card 4, which shows items for sale in a pet shop. It will help children discuss animals and will reinforce their understanding of plural nouns. The back of the card provides questions for children at various levels of language acquisition.
- In teams, children can present skits about shopping at the pet store. Guide children at all fluency levels to use gestures in their skits.

Self-Assessment

Have students think independently for a few minutes about what they learned from this unit. Suggest questions at the levels of content (*What did I learn about animals?*) and context (*How did I improve my English? What did I learn about handling everyday situations? What did I learn about working in school with others?*). Encourage students to think of other questions to ask themselves and others. Then have them come together in groups of three to five and discuss their questions and answers.

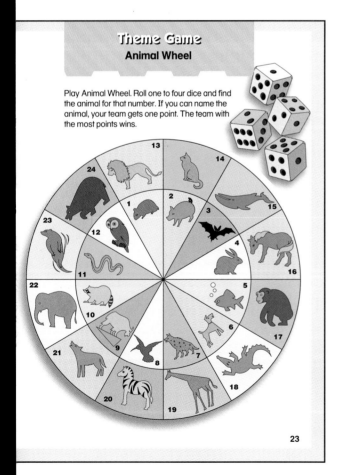

Theme Game
Animal Wheel

Play Animal Wheel. Roll one to four dice and find the animal for that number. If you can name the animal, your team gets one point. The team with the most points wins.

23

Story Card 4

Theme Bibliography

- Clément, Claude. *The Painter and the Wild Swans*. Dial Books, 1986. A Japanese painter is mesmerized by the beauty of a flock of wild swans. He puts away his brushes and cannot paint until he finds them again.

- Clutton-Brock, Juliet. *Dog*. Eyewitness Books Series, Alfred A. Knopf, 1991. The history of dogs, including information about behavior, breeds, and training, is beautifully presented.

- Cole, William, compiler. *A Zooful of Animals*. Houghton Mifflin, 1992. More than forty of the funniest poems about animals, from those written by Rudyard Kipling to those written by John Ciardi, are contained in this appealing, colorfully illustrated book.

- Evans, Mark. *Birds*. ASPCA Pet Care Guides for Kids. Dorling Kindersley, Inc., 1993. This excellent guide for young bird owners discusses how to prepare a bird's cage and how to care for a bird. Other titles in the series: *Kitten, Puppy, Rabbit, Guinea Pig*.

- Few, Roger. *Animal Encyclopedia for Children*. Macmillan, 1991. Filled with color photographs, drawings, maps, and diagrams, this book is organized into nine of Earth's habitats. For example, ice caps and tundras, coniferous forests, and other habitats are described. Included is a description of the animals found in each habitat.

- Kipling, Rudyard. *The Complete Just So Stories*. Viking, 1993. These classic animal stories about such subjects as why the elephant has a long trunk and how the whale got its special throat have been delightfully retold in this well-illustrated book.

- Kuklin, Susan. *Taking My Cat to the Vet*. Bradbury Press, 1988. Using full-color photographs, this helpful book takes a look at the real-life experience of taking a trip to the vet.

- Lauber, Patricia. *An Octopus Is Amazing*. Thomas Y. Crowell, 1990. This fascinating story is about a curiosity of the deep. The octopus is clever, resourceful, and in a word— *amazing*.

- Selsam, Millicent E. *Night Animals*. Four Winds Press, 1979. The activities of many familiar nocturnal animals are described in this beautifully photographed book.

- Sheldon, Dyan. *The Whales' Song*. Dial Books for Young Readers, 1991. After listening to her grandmother's story of seeing whales and hearing their songs many years ago, a young girl wants to see them and hear their singing.

- Yoshida, Toshi. *Rhinoceros Mother*. Philomel, 1991. Mother rhinoceros is wounded while protecting her baby. If the wound becomes infected, she will die. Help comes from an unexpected source.

See also the Professional Bibliography in the Teacher's Companion.

PRENTICE HALL REGENTS
A VIACOM COMPANY

© 1996 by Prentice Hall Regents
Prentice Hall Inc.
A Viacom Company
Upper Saddle River, NJ 07458

Printed in the United States of America

10 9 8 7 6 5 4 3 2

ISBN 0-13-368440-7

Prentice-Hall International (UK) Limited, London
Prentice-Hall of Australia Pty. Limited, Sydney
Prentice-Hall Canada Inc., Toronto
Prentice-Hall Hispanoamerican, SA., Mexico
Prentice-Hall of India Private Limited, New Delhi
Prentice-Hall of Japan, Inc., Tokyo
Simon & Schuster Asia Pte. Ltd., Singapore
Editora Prentice-Hall do Brasil, Ltda., Rio de Janeiro

Prentice Hall Regents
Publisher: Marilyn Lindgren
Development Editors: Carol Callahan, Fredrik Liljeblad, Kathleen Ossip
Assistant Editor: Susan Frankle
Director of Production: Aliza Greenblatt
Manufacturing Buyer: Dave Dickey
Production Coordinator: Ken Liao
Marketing Manager: Richard Seltzer

Editorial, Design, Production and Packaging
McClanahan & Company, Inc.

Project Director: Susan Cornell Poskanzer
Creative Director: Lisa Olsson
Design Director: Toby Carson
Director of Production: Karen Pekarne

TEACHERS EDITION
Illustration: Carlos Ochagaria, cover; Dartmouth Publishing p1

STORY CARDS
Illustration: Barbara Gray SC1; Jim Carson SC2; Fran Lee SC3; Shelley Dieterichs SC4

THEME POSTER
Illustration: Ann Neumann

Reduced Student Book art is credited in Student Book.